KidSparks
READING

Grade 3 Skillbook

Grade 3 Reading Skillbook
©2000 by TREND enterprises, Inc.
KidSparks™ is the registered trademark of TREND enterprises, Inc.

All rights reserved. No part of this publication may be reproduced or transmitted in any form
or by any means, electronic or mechanical, including photocopying, recording, or any information
storage and retrieval system, without permission from the publisher. For additional information,
write to TREND enterprises, Inc., P.O. Box 64073, St. Paul, MN 55164 U.S.A.

Printed in the United States of America

Rita C. Welch—Writer
Lynae Wingate—Editor
Mark Engblom—Designer

ISBN 1-889319-65-1

10 9 8 7 6 5

Reading Around the World

Skill: Contractions

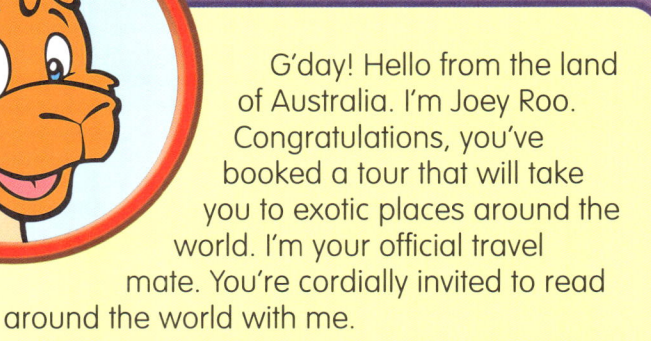

G'day! Hello from the land of Australia. I'm Joey Roo. Congratulations, you've booked a tour that will take you to exotic places around the world. I'm your official travel mate. You're cordially invited to read around the world with me.

Your Around-the-World Reading Tour begins in my island home, Australia. I'm so excited to introduce you to the beautiful grasslands where I graze and to meet some of my mates from the land down under.

From Australia, we travel across the ocean to the continent of Africa. After discovering the secrets of the desert, we'll play with Fennec Fox in his Sahara sandbox.

At the top of the globe, you'll enter the arctic world to visit the frozen tundra. There we've got time to spend with an arctic wolf pack.

From the North Pole, we travel to the beautiful forests near the Great Lakes. I'll take you to meet the King of the Northwoods, my mate, the moose.

From grasslands, to deserts, to tundra, to forests, reading is your passport to the world. Let's begin our journey!

Your travel mate,

Joey Roo

Contraction Action

Play a scavenger hunt game. Underline the contractions in Joey's letter. Write the two words that the contractions make. Challenge: Write some other contractions.

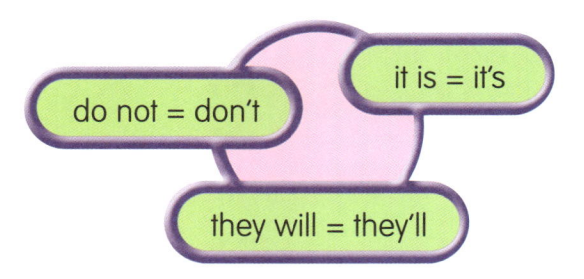

do not = don't
it is = it's
they will = they'll

BONUS: Form a book club. Write invitational letters to your friends. Travel together on the Around-the-World Reading Tour.

Reading Skillbook
©2000 TREND enterprises, Inc.

Prediction Puzzle

Skills: Making predictions, Story elements

Read the book titles and look at the pictures. What do you think will happen in each of the stories? Who are the characters? What is the setting? What do you think will happen in the reading selection? What questions do you think will be answered when you read the story?

Create-a-Clue Puzzle

Draw lines to connect a naming part and a telling part to create a sentence. Each sentence provides a clue about your Around-the-World Reading Tour adventures.

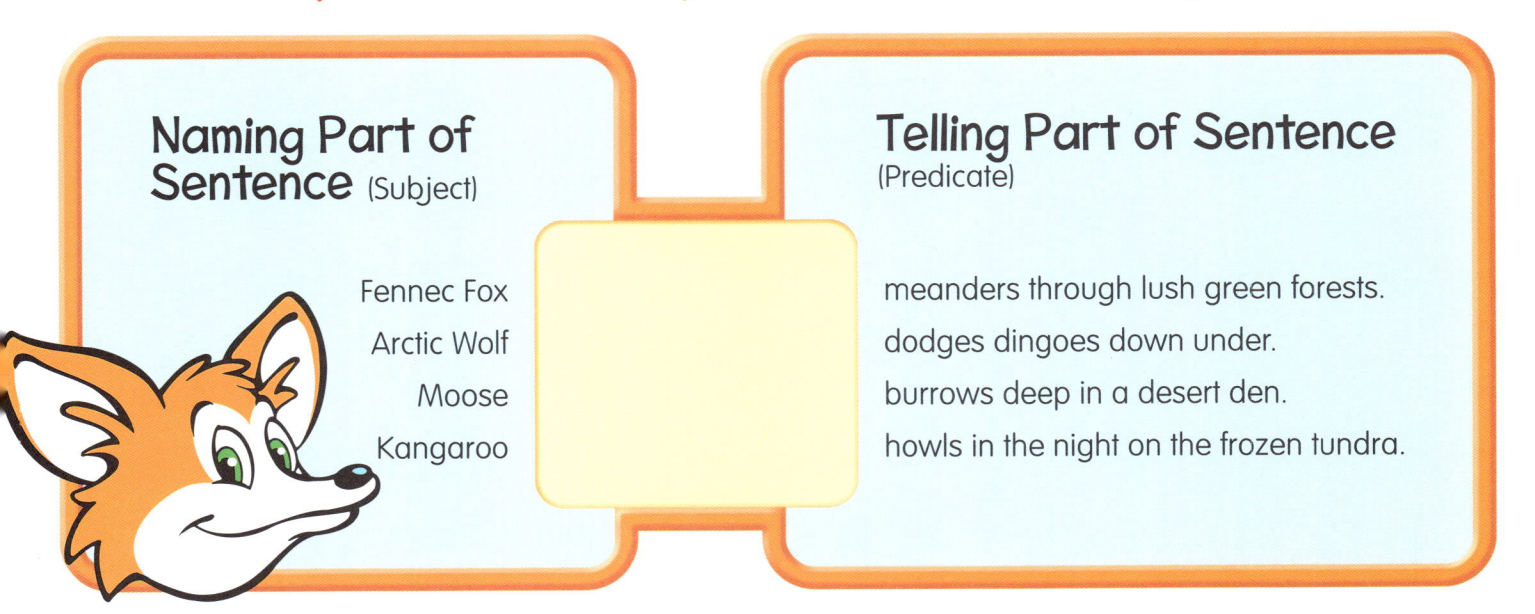

Naming Part of Sentence (Subject)

Fennec Fox
Arctic Wolf
Moose
Kangaroo

Telling Part of Sentence (Predicate)

meanders through lush green forests.
dodges dingoes down under.
burrows deep in a desert den.
howls in the night on the frozen tundra.

Reading Skillbook

©2000 TREND enterprises, Inc.

Oz Down Under

Welcome to AUSTRALIA!

Aussies call their beautiful homeland Oz. Australia is the world's largest island. Australia is the world's smallest continent. No other continent in the world is a single country.

To find this wondrous island continent, look down under the equator on a map or globe. The land down under was once connected to Asia. It was a part of a supercontinent, called Gondwanaland. Australia became an island when water covered the connecting bridge of land to Asia. The Pacific and Indian Oceans surround Australia.

Because Australia grew separately from other continents, many of its plants and animals are unique. Nowhere else on earth will you find kangaroos, wombats, and koalas in their natural habitats.

What does the land of Oz look like?

Australia is a land of immense deserts; low, flat grasslands; low mountain ranges; and sandy coastline beaches. This island is the flattest of all continents. Due to very little rain, it is the second driest continent.

The dry interior, known as the outback, has more sheep and cattle than people. Sheep and cattle stations can reach out for hundreds of miles. Imagine visiting your nearest neighbor by plane!

The north and east coasts of Australia are green and lush. Coastal cities sprouted up near beautiful sandy seashores. A range of mountains runs along the east coast. The Great Dividing Range is not very high or steep when compared to other mountains around the world.

The vast grasslands of Australia are grazing grounds for the island's famous kangaroos. Aussies call them roos.

Fun Facts

1. In Australia, the summer months are November through January. Winter is June through August. These seasons are the opposite of North America. School children in Australia have summer vacation during the Christmas and New Year's holiday season.

2. Australia's national holiday that is similar to the United States Independence Day falls on January 26.

3. Daytime in North America is Australia's nighttime.

Reading Skillbook

©2000 TREND enterprises, Inc.

Skill: Main ideas and details

Using the information from page 4, write sentences that describe the landscape, animals, and fun facts of Australia.

Landscape

_____
_____
_____
_____

Animals

_____
_____
_____
_____

Fun Facts

_____
_____
_____
_____

BONUS Find out more information about Australia. Does Australia have active volcanoes? Who are the Aborigines? What are the two Australian animals that are the only mammals in the world that hatch from eggs?

Reading Skillbook ©2000 TREND enterprises, Inc.

Kangaroo Facts and Fun

Kangaroo Facts

Marsupials (mar-soo-pe-uls) are animals with a pouch. Kangaroos are well-known marsupials who care for their young in a pouch. A young kangaroo is called a joey.

Kangaroos are mammals. They are warm-blooded animals. Joeys are born alive and feed on their mother's milk. This amazing marsupial lives in open grassy areas and wooded areas. Kangaroos are herbivores (ur-bu-vors), which means they eat only plants. They travel the open fields and woodlands of Australia grazing on green grasses and other plants.

Kangaroos live in groups called herds or mobs. Kangaroo families protect each other from danger. Dingoes are wild dogs that attack kangaroos. When a kangaroo senses this wild predator, she stands up and stomps her back feet. The kangaroo warns her family about the danger. The herd travels quickly to escape the dangerous dingo.

Other marsupials that live in Australia include koalas, wombats, opossums, and wallabies. The opossum is the only marsupial that can be found in North America.

Reading Skillbook

©2000 TREND enterprises, Inc.

Skills: Facts from nonfiction, Poetry

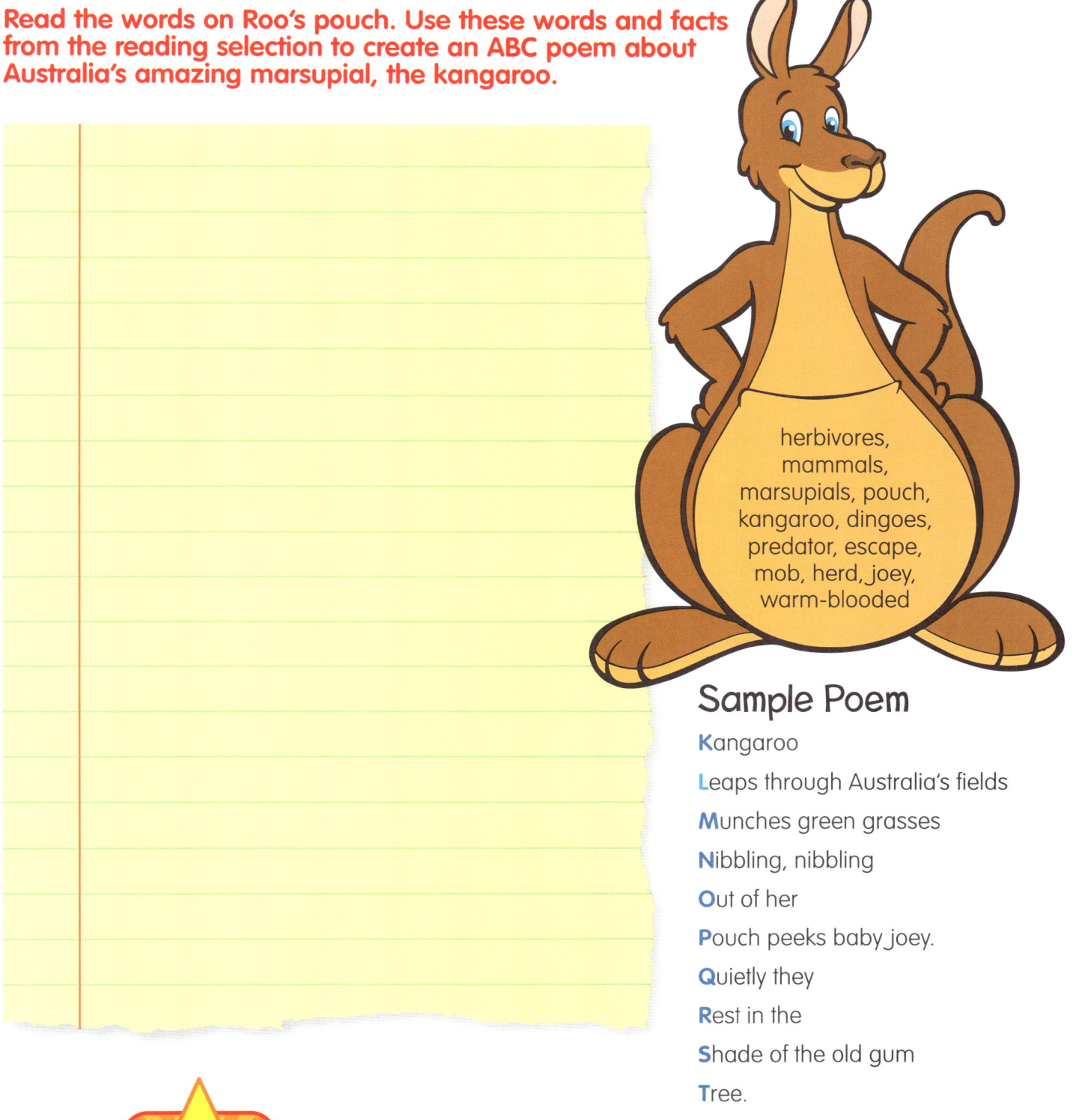

Read the words on Roo's pouch. Use these words and facts from the reading selection to create an ABC poem about Australia's amazing marsupial, the kangaroo.

herbivores, mammals, marsupials, pouch, kangaroo, dingoes, predator, escape, mob, herd, joey, warm-blooded

Sample Poem

Kangaroo

Leaps through Australia's fields

Munches green grasses

Nibbling, nibbling

Out of her

Pouch peeks baby joey.

Quietly they

Rest in the

Shade of the old gum

Tree.

BONUS

Research facts about other mammals, herbivores, or marsupials. Write an ABC poem about other amazing animals.

Reading Skillbook

©2000 TREND enterprises, Inc.

Runaway Joey Roo

HEY, THIS STORY IS ABOUT ME! WHO PUT THIS STORY IN THE BOOK?

Once upon a time in a land called Oz, there lived a young and curious kangaroo named Joey Roo. Early one morning as Joey grazed on grasses, he decided to hop away from home to seek adventure. "I want to see the world!" Joey exclaimed. Joey set off to find a travel mate.

Joey saw Emu sliding down the slippery dip at the playground. Joey asked, "Emu, will you be my travel mate?" Emu said, "Do you have a map so we don't get lost?" Joey said, "I hadn't thought of that."

Joey found Koala munching on eucalyptus (yu-kah-lip-tus) leaves. Joey asked, "Koala, will you be my travel mate?" Koala asked, "What if the wild dingoes attack us?" Joey said, "I hadn't thought of that."

Joey heard Kookaburra (kook-a-bur-ra) playing the didjeridoo (di-ju-ree-doo) in the old gum tree. Joey asked, "Kookaburra, will you be my travel mate?" Kookaburra said, "What if I miss the didjeridoo concert at the Billabong Band show?" Joey said, "I hadn't thought of that."

Joey saw Wombat munching on sweet lollies and freshly baked biscuits. Joey asked, "Wombat, will you be my travel mate?" Wombat said, "Won't our families miss us?" Joey said, "I hadn't thought of that."

Joey decided to start a book club instead of taking a faraway trip. He sent invitations to his friends Emu, Koala, Kookaburra, and Wombat. Each day after school, they met down near the billabong to read their way around the world.

Emu

Koala

Kookaburra

Wombat

Reading Skillbook

Skills: Story elements, Main idea and supporting details

Complete the story map using details from the story.

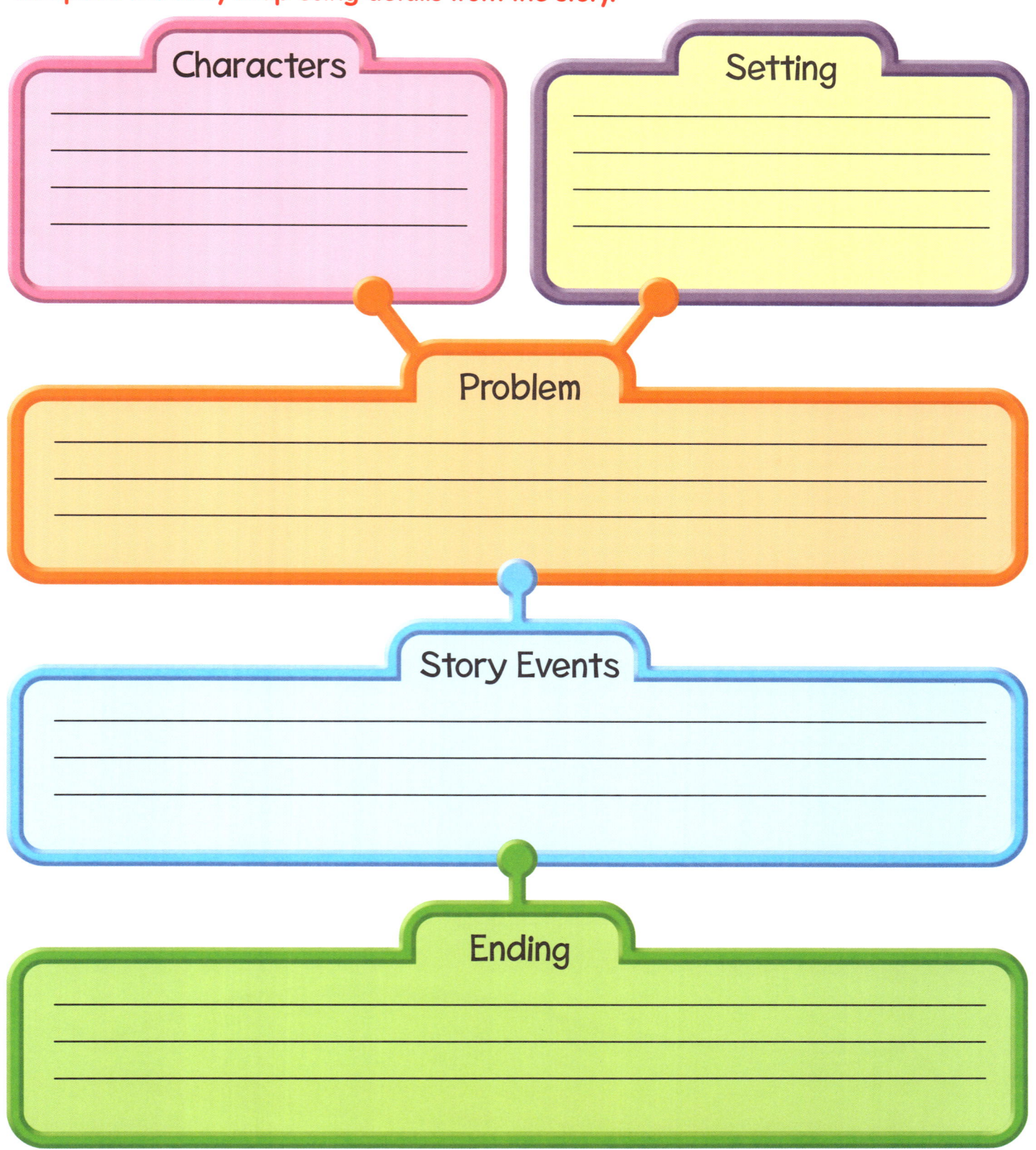

Characters
_____
_____
_____

Setting
_____
_____
_____

Problem
_____
_____
_____

Story Events
_____
_____
_____

Ending
_____
_____
_____

Reading Skillbook

©2000 TREND enterprises, Inc.

Dictionary Down Under

In "Runaway Joey Roo" on page 8, there are many words that are used mainly in Australia. Find the words from the Word Bank in Joey's story. Discover what they mean and write the word on the line below with its meaning.

Word Bank

Billabong   Lollies
Didjeridoo   Slippery Dip
Biscuits

_____ water hole

_____ playground slide

_____ musical instrument

_____ candy

_____ cookies

Reading Skillbook

©2000 TREND enterprises, Inc.

Skills: Using context clues, Vocabulary, Creative writing

Before you leave the beautiful island continent of Australia, think about the facts you've learned, the animals you've met, and the new words you can use from the Land of Oz.

Create your own travel tale or write a journal entry about Australia.

Australia

Reading Skillbook

©2000 TREND enterprises, Inc.

Nomad's Journal

My Desert Days

Each day I wake and behold the beauty of my homeland. I live in the largest desert in the world, the magnificent Sahara. My desert reaches from one side of North Africa to the other. I am Nomad. I wander from place to place searching out mysteries hidden in the desert. I must observe carefully to uncover the secrets of the Sahara.

At dawn, I gazed at the sun's rays chasing night shadows away from sand dunes. I glanced at a hawk spreading his wings wide overhead. As I wandered through the wadi, a dried up riverbed, I watched waltzing jinns dance with tumbleweeds. Waltzing jinns are like small whirls of wind. Near an oasis, I noticed spears of green yucca leaves waving up from the sand.

At midday the sun burned hot. I rested under the shade of date palm trees. The trees were like a canopy that blocked out the blazing sun.

Late in the afternoon, I spied a row of widely spaced flowers. The petals bowed with the breezes that swept over their heads. Grains of sand shifted under my feet. I looked out over the ripple patterns created by wind currents. My desert home is an endless sea of sunbaked sand. Waves of sand dunes reach up toward the sky.

Near sunset, I peered at barren rocks, black against the red-gold blaze. The sky became a canvas. The sun was the artist who filled the canvas with color. The rock formations were like shadow statues posing for a camera. Near a sturdy bush, I spotted small tracks. I studied the bush to find signs of burrowed dens of desert creatures.

At nightfall, the temperature drops. Night in my home can be very cold. Time for sleep. Tomorrow is another day to discover more Sahara secrets.

BONUS: Who do you think Nomad is? Look up information about the Sahara Desert to find out what kinds of creatures live there.

Skills: Vocabulary, Synonyms, Alphabetizing

Synonyms are words that have similar meanings.

Circle the synonyms for the word "look" in "My Desert Days." Then write each synonym below. Use a thesaurus to add other synonyms to your list.

LOOK

Put all the synonyms you find for "look" in alphabetical order.

1. _____
2. _____
3. _____
4. _____
5. _____
6. _____
7. _____
8. _____
9. _____
10. _____
11. _____
12. _____

BONUS

Take a walking tour near your home. Write a journal page that describes your neighborhood. Use the synonyms for the word "look" in your journal entry.

Reading Skillbook

©2000 TREND enterprises, Inc.

Word Safari

Skills: Figurative language, Personification

Authors use figurative language to help readers paint pictures in their minds as they read.

"The sun's rays chased away night shadows."

This sentence is an example of personification (per-sah-ni-fi-ka-shun). The author wanted the reader to imagine that the sun was a person chasing away shadows. When an author makes an object seem like a person, it is called personification.

On the lines, write sentences from "My Deserts Days" on page 12 that use personification to paint a strong picture for the reader.

_____
_____
_____
_____
_____
_____
_____
_____
_____

BONUS Find sentences that use personification to paint pictures. Write your own examples of personification.

Reading Skillbook

©2000 TREND enterprises, Inc.

Answers

Reading Grade 3

Page 2

Reading Around the World

Contraction Action

G'day! Hello from the land of Australia. I'm Joey Roo. Congratulations, you've booked a tour that will take you to exotic places around the world. I'm your official travel mate. You're cordially invited to read around the world with me.

Your Around-the-World Reading Tour begins in my island home, Australia. I'm so excited to introduce you to the beautiful grasslands where I graze and to meet some of my mates from the land down under.

From Australia, we travel across the ocean to the continent of Africa. After discovering the secrets of the desert, we'll play with Fennec Fox in his Sahara sandbox.

At the top of the globe, you'll enter the Arctic world to visit the frozen tundra. There we've got time to spend with an arctic wolf pack.

From the North Pole, we travel to the beautiful forests near the Great Lakes. I'll take you to meet the King of the Northwoods, my mate, the moose.

From grasslands, to deserts, to tundra, to forests, reading is your passport to the world. Let's begin our journey!

Your travel mate,
Joey Roo

G'day	=	Good day
I'm	=	I am
You're	=	you are
we'll	=	we will
you'll	=	you will
we've	=	we have
I'll	=	I will
Let's	=	let us

Page 3

Create-a-Clue Puzzle

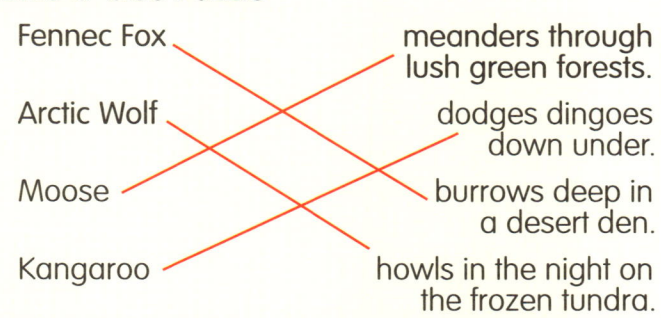

- Fennec Fox — burrows deep in a desert den.
- Arctic Wolf — howls in the night on the frozen tundra.
- Moose — meanders through lush green forests.
- Kangaroo — dodges dingoes down under.

Pages 4-5

Oz Down Under

Answers will vary. Examples are:

Landscape
Australia has immense deserts and low, flat grasslands.

Animals
Australia has unique animals like kangaroos, wombats, and koalas.

Fun Facts
Australia's summer is the opposite of North America.

Pages 6-7

Kangaroo Facts and Fun
Answers will vary. Make sure the first letter of each line is in alphabetical order like the sample poem.

Pages 8-9

Runaway Joey Roo
Answers will vary.

Characters Joey Roo, Emu, Koala, Kookaburra, Wombat

Setting The land of Oz (Australia)

Problem Joey Roo wants to see the world.

Story Events Joey asks his friends if they want to travel with him to see the world. Each friend has a reason why he or she can't go.

Ending Joey decides to start a book club instead of taking a faraway trip.

Reading Skillbook

©2000 TREND enterprises, Inc

Answers

Reading Grade 3

Pages 10-11

Dictionary Down Under

Word Bank

Billabong — water hole
Slippery Dip — playground slide
Didjeridoo — musical instrument
Lollies — candy
Biscuits — cookies

Australia Travel Tale
Answers will vary.

Pages 12-13

Nomad's Journal.

My Desert Days

Each day I wake and *behold* the beauty of my homeland. I live in the largest desert in the world, the magnificent Sahara. My desert reaches from one side of North Africa to the other. I am Nomad. I wander from place to place *searching* out mysteries hidden in the desert. I must *observe* carefully to uncover the secrets of the Sahara.

At dawn, I *gazed* at the sun's rays chasing night shadows away from sand dunes. I *glanced* at a hawk spreading his wings wide overhead. As I wandered through the wadi, a dried up riverbed, I *watched* waltzing jinns dance with tumbleweeds. Waltzing jinns are like small whirls of wind. Near an oasis, I *noticed* spears of green yucca leaves waving up from the sand.

At midday the sun burned hot. I rested under the shade of date palm trees. The trees were like a canopy that blocked out the blazing sun.

Late in the afternoon, I *spied* a row of widely spaced flowers. The petals bowed with the breezes that swept over their heads. Grains of sand shifted under my feet. I *looked out* over the ripple patterns created by wind currents. My desert home is an endless sea of sunbaked sand. Waves of sand dunes reach up toward the sky.

Near sunset, I *peered* at barren rocks, black against the red-gold blaze. The sky became a canvas. The sun was the artist who filled the canvas with color. The rock formations were like shadow statues posing for a camera. Near a sturdy bush, I *spotted* small tracks. I *studied* the bush to find signs of burrowed dens of desert creatures.

At nightfall, the temperature drops. Night in my home can be very cold. Time for sleep. Tomorrow is another day to discover more Sahara secrets.

Synonyms for Look

1. behold
2. gazed
3. glanced
4. looked out
5. noticed
6. observe
7. peered
8. searching
9. spied
10. spotted
11. studied
12. watched

Pages 14-15

Word Safari.
Answers may vary.

Personification
I watched waltzing jinns dance with tumbleweeds.
Near an oasis, I noticed spears of green yucca leaves waving up from the sand.
The petals bowed with the breezes that swept over their heads.

Similes
Waltzing jinns are small whirls of wind.
The trees were like a canopy that blocked out the blazing sun.
The rock formations were like shadow statues posing for a camera.

Metaphors
My desert home is an endless sea of sunblocked sand.
The sky became a canvas.
The sun was the artist who filled the canvas with color.

Answers

Reading Grade 3

Pages 16-17

Little Fox on the Sahara Story

Answers will vary.

Pages 18-19

Frozen Frontier KWL chart

Answers will vary. Examples are:

What I Know
It's cold at the Arctic Circle.
The Arctic Circle has three parts: the polar ice cap, the taiga, and the tundra.
The polar ice cap is the frozen ocean.

What I Want to Know
Do people live at the Arctic Circle?
What would happen if the ice melted?

Where I Will Look for Facts
Encyclopedia
Internet
Books from the library

Pages 20-21

Night Howl

Answers will vary. Examples are:

wolf
arctic   tundra
white   snowy   fur
omnivores   meat   and   plants
alpha   parents   lead   the   pack
wolf   talk   whines   barks   yelps   howls

Pages 22-23

King of the Northwoods

The King of the Northwoods
Wears an antler crown.
His coat of fur
Is chocolate <u>brown</u>.
He stands tall and proud
Above the <u>crowd</u>.
Moving gracefully through forest trees
On tall stilt legs with knobby <u>knees</u>.
This royal hoof prince leaves
Teardrop tracks,
Fighting other bull moose
Clashing <u>racks</u>.
Ready to duel for ladylove
With antler racks from <u>above</u>.
His dewlap beard hangs from his chin,
Droopy nose and tail that's <u>thin</u>.
The King of the Northwoods
Wears an antler crown.
His coat of fur
Is chocolate brown.

Pages 24-25

Moose Comics

Answers will vary. Examples are:

I have a wide rack of antlers.
My legs are skinny and my knees are knobby.
My tracks look like teardrops.
I have a dewlap beard under my chin.
I'm a moose calf.
I like to eat twigs, green leaves and tree bark
I can grow as high as seven feet!

Reading Skillbook

©2000 TREND enterprises, Inc

Answers

Reading Grade 3

Pages 26-27

Joey's Reading Survey

1) Animal Stories
2) Fantasy Stories
3) Science Fact Books and Poetry Books got 5 votes
4) 2 votes

Favorite Books of My Around-the-World Friends

Write sentences to describe the information in the graph.

Answers will vary. Examples are:

Joey's friends liked animal stories and tall tales the most.
Joey's friends liked fantasy stories and adventures the least.

Reading Skillbook

©2000 TREND enterprises, Inc

Word Safari

Skill: Similes and metaphors

Another way authors paint pictures for readers is to compare an object to something else.

Simile

A simile compares two things using the words "as" or "like."

"The desert is like a vast sea of sand."

The desert is compared to the sea. The word "like" is used to make the comparison.

Metaphor

A metaphor compares two things without using the words "as" or "like."

"The desert is a vast sea of sand."

The desert isn't really a sea, but it is compared to the sea. The words "like" or "as" are not used to make the comparison.

Find similes and metaphors in "My Deserts Days" on page 12. Write the sentences on the blanks below.

Similes

Metaphors

Reading Skillbook

©2000 TREND enterprises, Inc.

Little Fox on the Sahara

Welcome to my Sahara sandbox! I am Fennec. I am a desert fox who lives in Northern Africa. Fennecs are the smallest foxes in the world.

I look like a tiny fox. I weigh only about $3\frac{1}{2}$ pounds. My black eyes look like buttons. I have a bushy tail. My sandy-colored fur helps me hide in the desert. I can easily hide from other animals that would like to have me for dinner. You can easily spot a fennec by its ears. Although I am a very small fox, I have big bat ears.

My ears are like radiators. They release heat from my body so that I can keep cool in the desert. My ears help me hear the tiniest noises. If I listen carefully, I hear small insects and rodents that are scurrying deep down in the sand. Yummy! Dinner!

I am nocturnal. During the hot daytime hours, my family and I snuggle down in our burrowed home. Our desert den tunnels down deep in the sand. Sometimes my brothers and I like to peek out of the den's entrance. If the coast is clear, we play around the sturdy shrub that hides our home. When you visit the desert, you may see signs of our playground games. We like to leave paw-print tracks in the sand. Sometimes our fur catches on the branches of bushes.

At night, my parents take turns hunting for food. I wait anxiously at the den door for dinner to arrive. Soon I will learn how to hunt at night for food. For now, I'll enjoy being a kit, playing in my Sahara sandbox.

BONUS: Check out informational books from your library to find out more about the fascinating fennec fox.

Skills: Story elements, Vocabulary skills

Use the facts you've learned about fennec foxes to create a fictional story. Plan your story by writing your ideas in the sand castle.

Who are your characters?
_____
_____
_____
_____
_____

What is your setting?
_____
_____
_____
_____
_____

What is the problem to be solved?
_____
_____
_____
_____

What is the solution to the problem?
_____
_____
_____
_____
_____

Reading Skillbook
©2000 TREND enterprises, inc.

Frozen Frontier

Brrr! It's cold up here at the top of the world! Imagine a circle around the top of the globe. This imaginary circle is called the Arctic Circle. This frozen frontier has three parts.

The **polar ice cap** is the frozen ocean with the North Pole at the center. In fact, the North Pole is called the arctic cap.

Over one thousand miles from the North Pole, tall evergreen trees grow. This tree-filled section is called the **taiga** (ti-gah).

Between the tree line and the polar ice cap, lies the frozen land called the **tundra**. This treeless, flat plain has long harsh winters and short summers. Only small, low-to-the-ground bushes survive the brutal winter winds. The earth below the surface of the ground is frozen even during the summer months. The frozen earth of the tundra is called permafrost.

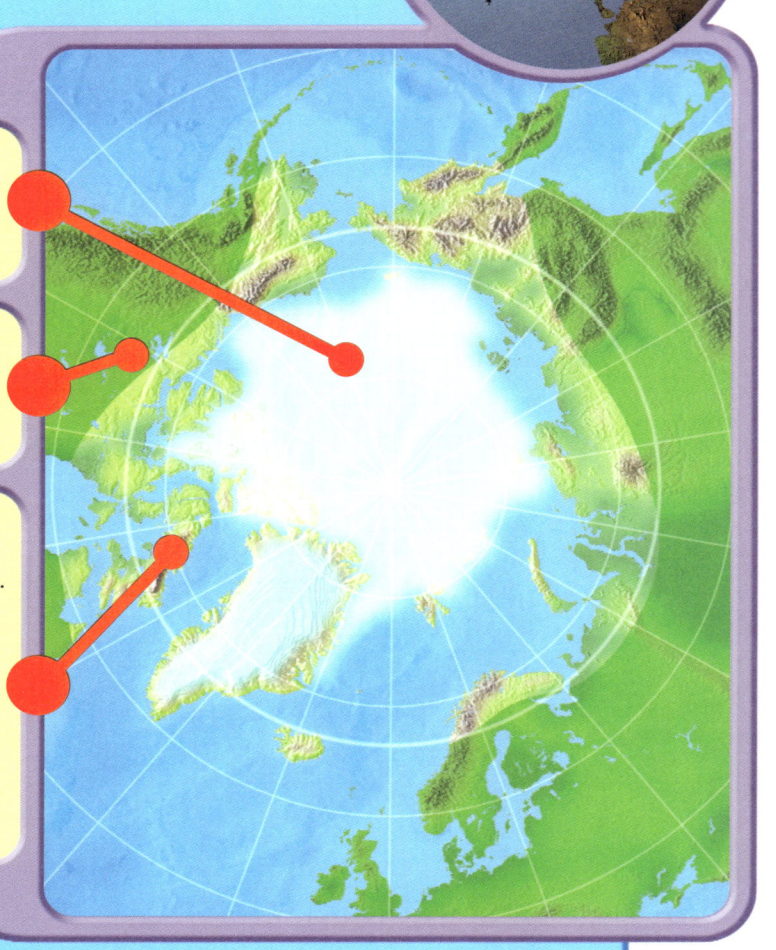

The tundra is home to many animals. Herds of caribou and reindeer roam the tundra. Arctic wolves and foxes also call the tundra home. Arctic animals have adapted to the challenges of living on the frozen frontier.

Research

Read books about the world of the Arctic Circle. Find out about Europe, Asia, and North America, the three places that border the Arctic Ocean. Learn about two arctic mysteries: aurora borealis and the midnight sun.

Reading Skillbook

©2000 TREND enterprises, Inc.

Skills: Comprehension, Research skills

Complete the KWL chart to prepare for more arctic research.

ARCTIC EXPRESS PRESS

Reporter _____

Frozen Frontier Facts	Question Quest	Research Round-Up
What I **Know**	What I **Want** to Know	Where I Will **Look** for Facts

Write fact sentences that describe what you KNOW about the Arctic Circle.

Write questions that describe what you WANT to know about the Arctic Circle.

Write ideas that describe where you will LOOK for more facts about the Arctic Circle.

Reading Skillbook

©2000 TREND enterprises, Inc.

Night Howl

Howwwl! Arctic Greetings

I'm Alpha, leader of my wolf pack. I live on the frozen tundra in the arctic. Look at the top of your globe to find my home.

Cool Camouflage

My coat of fur changes from gray to a creamy white during the winter. Having white fur helps me hide in snowy places. My enemies won't see me.

We Are Family

Wolves travel together in a pack.

My mate and I are the alpha leaders of the pack. We are the parents. We rule!

Omnivores? What's For Dinner?

Wolves are omnivores (ahm-ni-vors). We eat meat and plants. We hunt together for food to share. Of course, as the leader of the pack, I eat first.

Night Howls

Wolves are nocturnal. We hunt at night. Because our eyesight is poor, we use our powerful noses and ears to track down our prey.

Night Noises

Our yelps, barks, whines, and howls are wolf talk. We have our very own language.

Shy Guy

People sometimes fear wolves. We've gotten a bad rap in fairy tales and other children's stories. We are wild animals who need to live in our natural habitat. We actually like to be left alone. We shy away from humans.

Reading Skillbook ©2000 TREND enterprises, Inc.

Skills: Comprehension, Main ideas and details, Organizing facts

Follow the directions to create a Fact Pyramid for the arctic wolf.

Write one word to describe the animal in "Night Howl."

Write two words to describe the habitat of the arctic wolf.

Write three words to describe what the arctic wolf looks like.

Write four words to describe what the arctic wolf eats.

Write five words to describe the wolf's family life.

Write six words to describe a fun fact about the arctic wolf.

BONUS

Write a fairy tale about the arctic wolf. Will your character be a hero or a villain?

Reading Skillbook

©2000 TREND enterprises, Inc.

King of the Northwoods

Skills: Poetry, Rhyming words

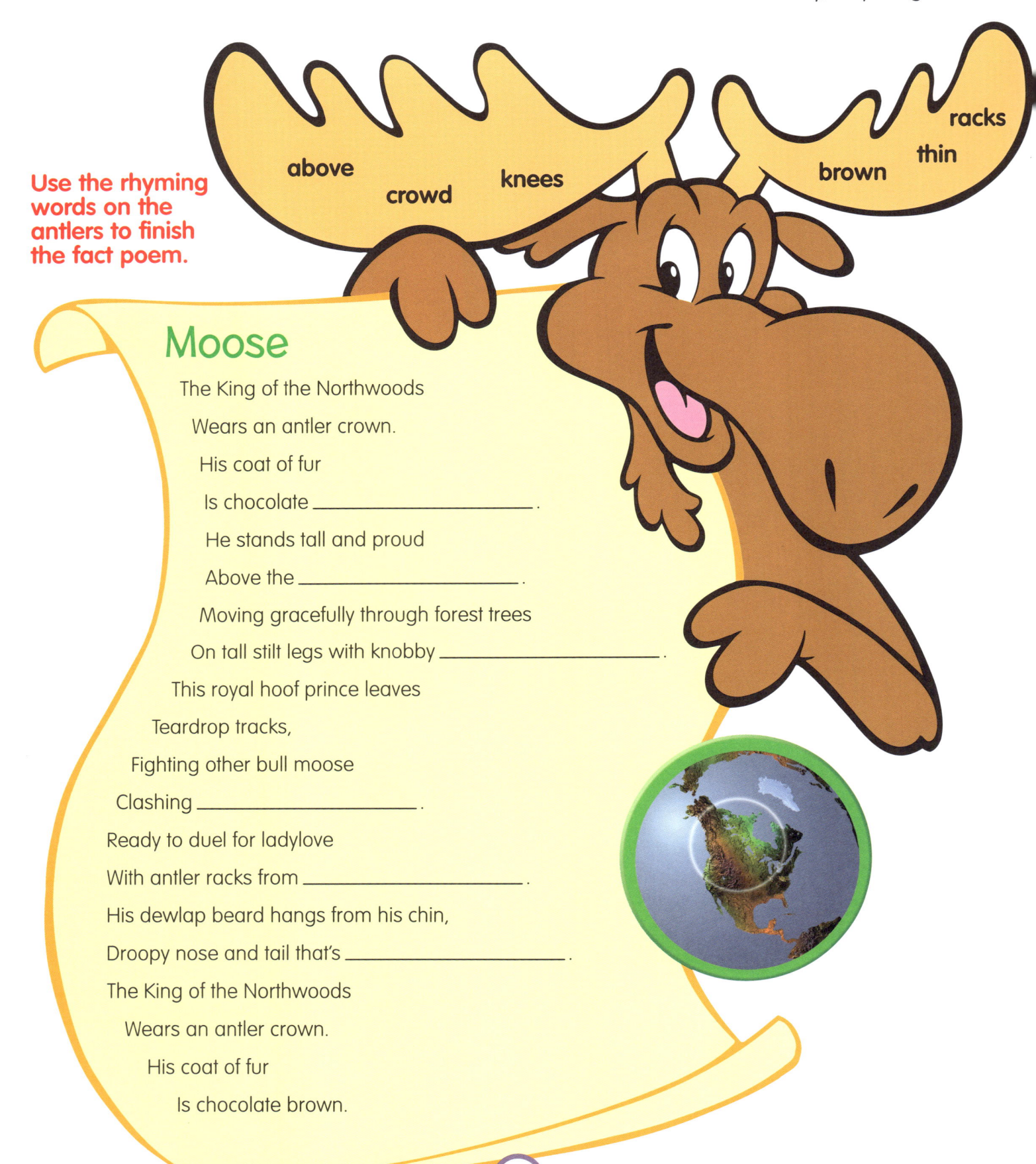

Use the rhyming words on the antlers to finish the fact poem.

Antler words: above, crowd, knees, brown, thin, racks

Moose

The King of the Northwoods

Wears an antler crown.

His coat of fur

Is chocolate _____.

He stands tall and proud

Above the _____.

Moving gracefully through forest trees

On tall stilt legs with knobby _____.

This royal hoof prince leaves

Teardrop tracks,

Fighting other bull moose

Clashing _____.

Ready to duel for ladylove

With antler racks from _____.

His dewlap beard hangs from his chin,

Droopy nose and tail that's _____.

The King of the Northwoods

Wears an antler crown.

His coat of fur

Is chocolate brown.

Reading Skillbook

©2000 TREND enterprises, Inc.

Moose Facts

Skills: Reading a chart, Comprehension

Look at the pictures. Read the fun facts in the chart to learn about the moose.

	Looks like	brown fur, tall skinny legs, knobby knees, wide rack of antlers, dewlap beard under its chin, big droopy nose, tiny tail, largest member of the deer family
	Eats	twigs, green leaves, water lilies, tree bark, chews cud and stores food to eat all day long
	Habitat	forests spotted with lakes; Europe, Asia, North America
	Enemies	bear, wolf; defends itself by snorting loudly and kicking with strong legs
	Babies	calves grow as high as seven feet at the shoulder, males weigh up to 1,800 pounds

Reading Skillbook

©2000 TREND enterprises, Inc.

Moose Comics

Create a comic strip using the facts from the chart on page 23. Be sure to include ideas you've learned from the "King of the Northwoods" poem on page 22.

MOOSE COMICS   By _____

"GREETINGS FROM THE NORTHWOODS! I'M MOOSE, BUT YOU CAN CALL ME KING."

Reading Skillbook

24

©2000 TREND enterprises, Inc.

Skills: Interpreting a chart, Creative writing

BONUS Find the answers to these questions:
Do all moose have antlers? Do moose ever lose their antlers? What are antlers made of?

Joey's Reading Survey

Joey wanted to find out what kinds of books his around-the-world animal friends liked to read. He conducted a survey and asked this question: "What types of books do you like best?" Here are Joey's research notes.

Count the tally marks to answer the questions.

My Reading Survey

Favorite Books of My Around-the-World Friends

Type of Book	How Many Friends
Adventures	|||
Mysteries	||||
Tall Tales	|||||	
Animal Stories	||||| ||
Fantasy Stories	||
Science Fact Books	|||||
Poetry Books	|||||

1. Which type of book did the around-the-world friends like the best? _____

2. Which type of book did the around-the-world friends vote for the least? _____

3. Which types of books got the same number of votes? _____

4. How many more votes did Tall Tales get than Mysteries? _____

Reading Skillbook

©2000 TREND enterprises, Inc.

Skill: Interpreting data from charts and graphs

Help Joey organize his research notes. Color in the bar graph to show the results of his reading survey.

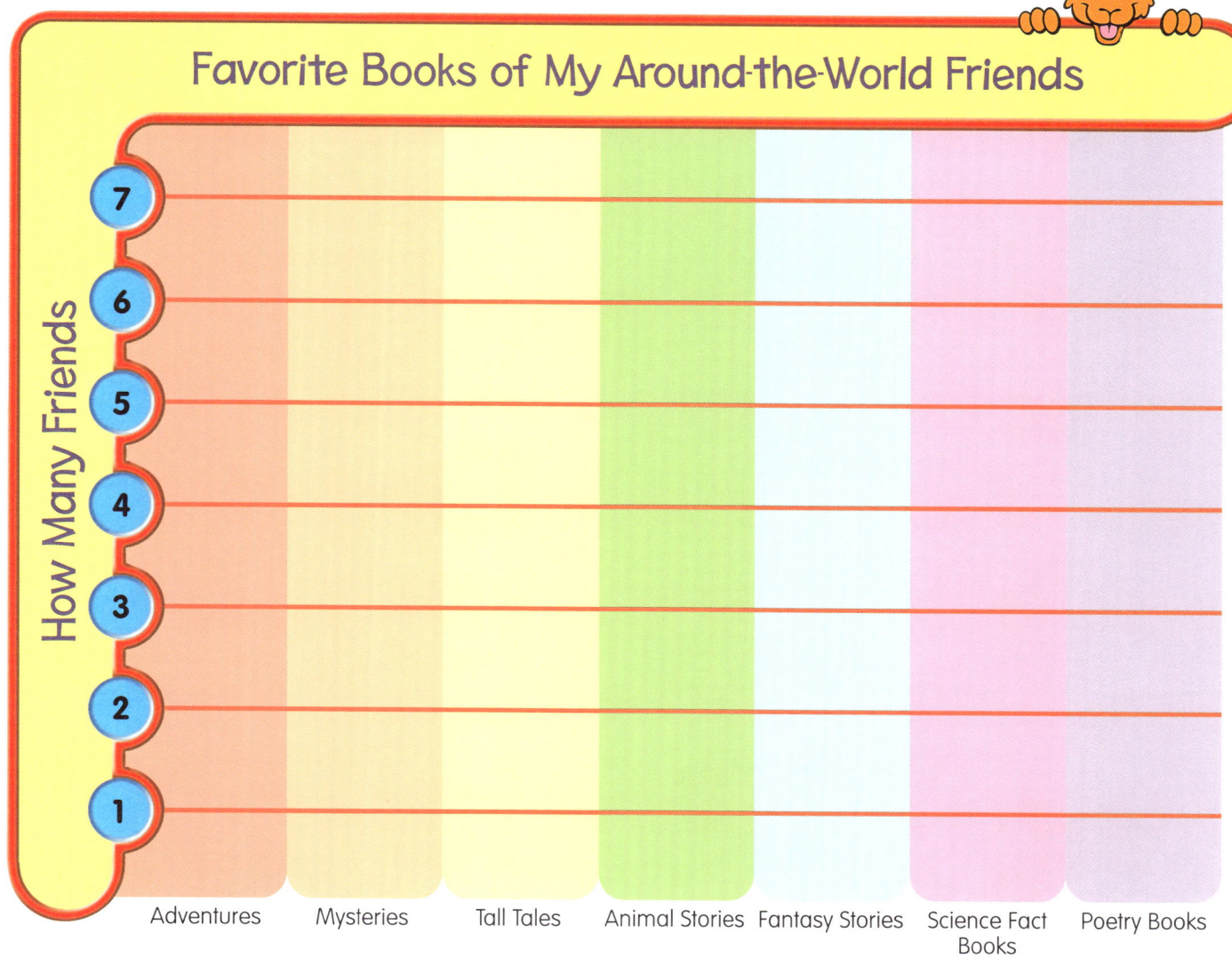

Favorite Books of My Around-the-World Friends

How Many Friends

7
6
5
4
3
2
1

Adventures   Mysteries   Tall Tales   Animal Stories   Fantasy Stories   Science Fact Books   Poetry Books

Write sentences to describe the information in the graph.

_____
_____
_____

BONUS

Conduct your own reading survey. Interview your friends, family, and classmates to find out what kinds of books they like to read. Make a bar graph to organize your survey results.

Reading Skillbook

©2000 TREND enterprises, Inc.

Around the World
Certificate of Reading

Presented to:

_____

Congratulations on your successful completion of the Around the World Reading Adventures.

Signature:

Joey Roo

Color the stamps for the selections you've read.

- ☐ Oz Down Under
- ☐ Kangaroo Facts and Fun
- ☐ Runaway Joey Roo
- ☐ My Desert Days
- ☐ Little Fox on the Sahara
- ☐ Frozen Frontier
- ☐ Night Howl
- ☐ King of the Northwoods

Reading Skillbook

©2000 TREND enterprises, Inc.